10 ridiculously simple tips series

Connecting Your
Business Plan

To A Modern World

Straightforward Information in Condensed Format

ARTISTIC / BUSINESS SERIES

created by John DeGaetano

ARTISTIC / BUSINESS SERIES
created by John DeGaetano

About the Series

The "*how to*" series is designed to give you straightforward information on a variety of subjects in a condensed format. These books help you be yourself, and guides your vision on the artistic/creative side of your personality as relates to a business setting. Most experts agree that for many art and passion finds it's way into the things we do, however to make it as an entrepreneur and do whatever it is you truly love, the art of business side comes into play… and vice versa. How you treat your business side of things is really the key to success.

About this Book

Connecting Your Business Plan to a Modern World touches on all the things you should consider in writing a business plan in today's changing world. Learn how to set goals for the business based on research and new tools available for small business owners. We'll give you 10 important "modern thinking" tips to consider along with style/guideline considerations as it relates to the various types of businesses.

Putting the Pieces Together

Starting-up, Then and Now: Is Business Life Better Today? Now more than ever before we are using technology, but has it helped us to be more engaging, innovative, and most importantly - profitable?
Customers are calling for more enhanced storylines, better product development, and faster diverse distribution channels. So building connections with the right people and businesses is a crucial part of being successful today.

This book helps participants become more familiar with writing, business planning, statistics, and understanding the obstacles we face - now, verses years past as today's world changes around us. Connect your business plan to modern markets with these well collected list of helpful "modern thinking" tips.

What does Wikipedia say?

Business Plan

A Business Plan is a formal statement of business goals, reasons they are attainable, and plans for reaching them. It may also contain background information about the organization or team attempting to reach those goals.

Business plans may target changes in perception and branding by the customer, client, taxpayer, or larger community. When the existing business is to assume a major change or when planning a new venture, a 3 to 5 year business plan is required, since investors will look for their investment return in that timeframe.

Business plans may be internally or externally focused. Externally focused plans target goals that are important to external stakeholders, particularly financial stakeholders. They typically have detailed information about the organization or team attempting to reach the goals. With or-profit entities, external stakeholders include investors and customers. External stakeholders of non-profits include donors, or government agencies, taxpayers, government agencies, and/or other international lending bodies.

Internally focused business plans target intermediate goals required to reach the external goals. They may cover the development of a new product, a new service, a new IT system, a restructuring of finance, the refurbishing of a factory or a restructuring of the organization. An internal business plan is often developed in conjunction with a balanced scorecard or a list of critical success factors. This allows success of the plan to be measured using non-financial measures. Business plans that identify and target internal goals, but provide only general guidance on how they will be met are called strategic plans.

Operational plans describe the goals of an internal organization, working group or department. Project plans, sometimes known as project frameworks, describe the goals of a particular project. They may also address the project's place within the organization's larger strategic goals.

*Information courtesy of Wikipedia, the free encyclopedia.

Interesting Facts

Writing a business plan and its value is often debated with entrepreneurs. Very successful businesses have been launched with a well-thought-out business plan, yet you can find equally successful ones that were launched in a garage somewhere with just a few raw notes.

However, statistics show that those who completed business plans were nearly twice as likely to successfully grow their businesses or obtain capital as those who didn't write a plan.

To be more specific, more than one third of them secured a loan or investment capital. And well over half of them have grown their business in the past five years. The numbers to success to businesses without a formal business plan amount to only half of those that do.

"Except in rare cases a small number of cases, all this research indicates that the type of entrepreneur who completes a business plan is also more likely to be a better entrepreneur and run a more successful business."

The popular reasons to start your own business;

- Personal achievement as their primary motivation for success or looking for financial stability.
- Got their idea from a previous job that inspired them.
- Interested at the same time in building skills in technology or other areas.
- Interested in the personal freedom of owning a business and potential growth associated with it.
- While others want to give back to their community and develop great business relationships.

So there you have it: you're better off and twice as likely to grow your business or achieve funding if you have taken the time to write a business plan.

<u>The Good News:</u> is… if you are willing to learn how to create an excellent business plan, with a little extra effort, you will usually get an even better response from prospective investors, financial institutions, community and customers alike.

Statistics

General Business Statistics
As a business owner, you will need a solid understanding of your market and current economic conditions to plan for business growth and success. The SBA Dept at sba.gov has a wealth of information to help you indentify your market and demographic information. The following resources provide statistics and reports on a variety of

U.S. industries and business conditions (information courtesy of the SBA Dept.)

North American Industry Classification System (NAICS Codes) – Provides the standard used by Federal statistical agencies in classifying business establishments for the purpose of collecting, analyzing and publishing statistical data related to the U.S. business economy. Information includes definition of each industry and background material.

FedStats – Offers a full range of official statistical information produced by more than 100 agencies. Site provides data and trend information on topics such as economic and population trends, crime, education, health care, aviation safety, energy use, farm production and more.

Statistical Abstract of the United States – Presents an authoritative and comprehensive summary of statistics on the social, political and economic conditions in the United States.

Statistics of U.S. Businesses – Features a collection of data files created from U.S. Census County Business Patterns, an annual series that provides sub-national economic data by industry.

So why is a plan so important? Answer: Economic Impact. Based on their records, the U.S. Bureau of Labor and Statistics summarizes a business chief goal is to attract, motivate and retain the most qualified employees and match them to jobs for which they are best suited. This translates into dollars and cents... ultimately, Economic Impact through reputation and planning.

Tips...

OK then, after your objectives are determined, prioritize the content of your business plan to suit those objectives. You have a small window of time to get the interest of an investor, landlord, banker, family member, etc so being detailed and extremely focused is essential. A lengthy business plan (over 40 pages) does not necessarily translate to higher potential of success; it may even encourage the reader to skim though or by pass the document just based on the sight of its length.

To successfully launch a truly great business plan, follow these helpful modern tips:

1. Draft a Business Summary of Ideas and Overviews

Creating a business summary not for the plan itself but for your own guidelines can be tricky, especially in the planning stages. These are the planning stages of your concept, a potential business model, an overview of where your business might lead.

If you already own an existing business, summarizing your current operation should be relatively easy; however it can be a lot harder task to decide what you plan to become.

So start by taking a step backward... and think outside the box. Then, answer a few questions:

- Who exactly are your customers?
- What products and services will you provide?
- And, what will you need to have in order to provide these items or services?

- When, in the form of a timeline will you provide these products or services?
- Where, demographically speaking are your customers?
- Why is there market or need for your business and is there a story to tell?
- How you will provide those products or services to your customer?

Let's Set The Stage

Tech and The Economy Just 20 Years Ago...

- The Search Engine Google is founded
- Apple Computer unveils the iMac
- U.S. Bancorp lowers its prime rate to 8.25%
- Worlds first Digital Terrestrial Television Service is launched
- Windows 98 released by Microsoft in June
- US Dept. of Justice brings Anti-Trust Case against Microsoft
- Technology starts to mature as E-commerce takes off
- Average Yearly Income $38,100, Average Monthly Rent $619.00

The World, Cost of Living, Etc.
Just 20 Years Ago...

- 19 European nations agree to forbid human cloning
- Bill Clinton Impeached for perjury and obstruction of justice
- India and Pakistan test nuclear weapons
- The FDA approves Viagra for use
- Average cost of new car $17,200
- Average Cost of new house $129,300
- Cost of a gallon of Gas $1.15
- Dozen Eggs 88 cents and 1 LB of Bacon $2.53
- US Postage Stamp 32 cents

(Source: thepeoplehistory.com)

For the NOW – A mix of Good, Bad, and Ugly

- Anti-immigration efforts effect workforce and Tax concerns
- The potential of a trade war and/or foreign policy concerns
- Incomes are rising and true well-being even more so
- Interest rates and inflation remain low
- Labor markets are tight, rising wages puts pressure on profits
- Exports and business investment is picking up
- There is a population shift to the west and south
- Housing will constrain growth in some areas
- Recent natural disasters effect economic pace
  (Source: beaconeconomics.com)

Running a Business is Not an Easy Gig

Business owners asked about running a Small business:

- 59% said its harder to run a business NOW, 30% said the same, 12% said THEN
- Small businesses who think its harder point to: 55% because of the economy, 49% said keeping pace with technology, and 40% said more competition

Three biggest difference in doing business THEN vs. NOW

- 84% Use more online marketing tools, 59% said economic uncertainty, 27% said use more automated solutions

So then, modern thinking is more important than ever... That in mind, we'll cover the following guidelines:

Connecting Your Business Plan *and* Modern Thinking Tips

1. Business Summary of Ideas and Overviews (page 12)
2. Business Name, Executive Summary
3. Mission Statement, Goals and Objectives
4. Organization/Business: Legal Structure, Permits/Licenses, Insurance
5. Organization/Business: Operations, Facility/Location, Equipment, Management/Personnel
6. Marketing Plan: Product/Service Description, Market Research, Target and Competitive Analysis
7. Marketing Plan: Pricing, Industry Trends, Marketing and Budget Planning
8. Financial Plan: Revenue and Expense Projections, Cash Flow, and Break-even Analysis
9. Financial Plan: Summary of Financial Needs, Managing Growth Historical, Business/Personal Credit Report Summary
10. Appendix: Timetable, Key Contacts, Resume, Samples: Marketing Materials or Concepts, Lease/Rental Agreements, Contracts

2. Executive Summary

The Executive Summary is a brief outline (1 to 3 pages) of the company's purpose and goals. A good Summary includes:

- A brief description of products and services
- A summary of objectives
- A solid description of the market
- A high-level justification for viability (including a look at your competition and your competitive advantage)
- A snapshot of growth potential
- An overview of funding requirements

The Executive Summary is usually the make-or-break "snapshot" section of the plan. A great business plan solves customer problems and shows how you'll make a profit.

The summary shows how you plan to take advantage of a genuine opportunity.

No "hype" or "sales pitch" here. Instead, focus on what you plan to do, how you plan to do it, and how you will succeed. A well-crafted summary is a good start to growing your business.

The Executive Summary serves as a guide to writing the rest of your plan and will first and foremost help to:

1. Refine and tighten your concept. Think of it as a written "elevator pitch" (w/ more detail, of course).
   - Describes the highlights of your plan, includes only the most critical points.
   - Leaves out less important issues and factors.

2. Determine priorities. Your business plan walks the reader through your vision. What ranks high in terms of importance? Product development? Research? Innovation? Acquiring the right location? Creating strategic partnerships?

In Review, include a:
   - Brief description of products/services.
   - A summary of objectives.
   - A solid description of the market.
   - A snapshot of viability, potential growth.
   - An overview of funding requirements.

Modern Thinking Tips
   - A snapshot of growth potential should always be supported by up-to-date analysis data for your business type.
   - Prove high-level justification for viability with the added use of online surveys and social feedback.

- Research competition in various markets and dig for several solid competitive advantages.
- Being virtual can build profits. Online collaboration is more common now more than ever for every operational application.
- In addition, 52% of US businesses save on overhead by being home-based. (Source: SBA 2014)

3. Mission Statement

The best example of a mission statement will define a company and its purpose in 30 seconds or less. This is an eloquent, concise paragraph that should be full of meaning and impact.

Choose your words wisely—beware of buzzwords, empty phrases, or mission statements that are so general they could apply to many different companies.

It's a challenge, but you want to capture what your company stands for in a brief and memorable way.

A Mission Statement should answer questions people have about your business, like:

- Who you are (your company)?
- What do you do?
- What do you stand for?
- And why do you do what you do?
- How you'll make a profit?
- What markets are served, and benefits offered?
- The problem you solve for customers?
- Internal work environment do you want for your employees?

Effective mission statements cover most of these points...

Developing a useful mission statement in five easy steps:
1. Start with your market-defining story
2. Define how your customer's life is better because your business exists
3. Consider what your business does for employees
4. Add what the business does for its owners
5 Discuss, review, get opinions, revise

In Review, include:
- Company and its purpose in 30 seconds or less.
- A paragraph filled with meaning and impact.
- Be specific to your industry.
- What your company stands for.
- Be memorable...

Modern Thinking Tips

- Approach planning as more of a "modern" art than a science

- Customers are calling on more enhanced storylines, better product development, and faster diverse distribution channels.
- Create an objectives framework that can accommodate regional or global change.
- Provide several payment methods to suit buyer's modern transaction habits and style.
- Connect with customers on a more personal level or something they can identify with through your statement.

4. Legal Structure, Permits/Licenses, Insurance

Sole Proprietorship - A sole proprietorship is the most basic type of business to establish. You alone own the company and are responsible for its assets and liabilities.

Liability Company - An LLC is designed to provide the limited liability features of a corporation and the tax efficiencies and operational flexibility of a partnership.

Cooperative - People form cooperatives to meet a collective need or to provide a service that benefits all member-owners.

Corporation - A corporation is more complex and generally suggested for larger, established companies with multiple employees.

Partnership - There are several different types of partnerships, which depend on the nature of the arrangement and partner responsibility for the business.

S Corporation - An S corporation is similar to a C corporation but you are taxed only on the personal level.

In Review:
- Choose the legal structure that is right for your business.
- Research online for permit and licensing requirements for your type of business and location.
- Nowadays you can discuss insurance with a broker for competitive quotes for coverage for your product and/or services.

Modern Thinking Tips

- Start small... Approx. two thirds of businesses start as sole proprietors and 64% of small business owners start with $10,000 or less.
- Use "Entity Choice Wizard" to compare different business formation options online to help you determine which one will suit your business best. Website: mycorporation.com
- Believe it or not, over 70 percent of U.S. businesses are owned and operated by sole proprietors.

- Today, there are 1.7 million traditional C corporations, compared to 7.4 million partnerships and S corporations... but 23 million are sole proprietorships. (Source: taxfoundation.com)

5. Facility/Location, Equipment and Management

This section details the investment needed to start or expand the business and the expected financial performance of the business for the next three years.

The first of those documents is a list of what resources (examples; building, machinery, equipment, etc.) will be needed to open or expand the business. It should also explain how the costs of these resources will be financed either by the owner or an outside source of financing. Details supporting these costs should be included in an appendix to the business plan.

Management Summary (*example of the summary*)

The two managers, Ace Contractors, Inc. owner (listed here) and General Operations Manager (name), have impeccable credentials previously in our industry (Profile history of each).

This will benefit our company in three ways:
1. Clients will be brought from existing professional relationships
2. Respect and recognition by associated organizations and state departments.
3. The experience each has will attract new clients in the area of finance and administration.

(*Example continued*) - A Training Manager will be finalized in the coming year and will also include a Sales Manager and Contractor from within the industry. Their extensive experience in management will provide a success.

Source of Funds and Use		
Source of Funds		
Owners and/or Other Investors	$	180,000
Bank Financing	$	200,000
Other Loans	$	50,000
Total Source of Funds	$	430,000
Use of Funding		
RealEstate/Buildings, Land, Etc	$	100,000
Leasehold Improvements	$	80,000
Capital for Equipment	$	80,000
Start-Up Inventory	$	25,000
Location and Admin Costs	$	18,000
Advertising & Promotional Costs	$	5,000
Other Expenses	$	2,000
Working Capital	$	100,000
Contingency Funds	$	20,000
Total Use of Funds	$	430,000

Personnel Plan (*example*)
By the end of June 2019, with the assumption of increased business volume, it will require that a Supervisor be added to our staff. By the end of August 2019, increased volume will require hiring additional staff in Operations.

In this example: Salaries of sales consultants, personnel, etc is included in the Cost of Sales. Only those costs for the hourly professional and administrative staff are shown in the Personnel table below.

	Year 1	Year 2	Year 3
Sales Consultants	$0	$10,000	$16,000
Operations Staff	$0	$40,000	$40,000
Trainers	$0	$0	$0
Additional Contractor(s)	$16,000	$32,000	$48,000
Admin Support	$10,000	$18,000	$28,000
Total Personnel	2	6	8
Total Payroll	$26,000	$100,000	$132,000

A Note on Personnel
Did You Know?
- • Small businesses provide 55% of all jobs, and 66% of all net new jobs since the 1970's. (Source: SBA 2017)
- • 86.3% of small business owners said they take a yearly salary of less than $100k. 30.07% of small business owners don't take a salary. (Source: Fundera)
- It takes an average of 27 days to hire a new employee. The best candidates are off the market within 10 days. (Source: Undercover Recruiter)

In Review:

- Detail the investment needed to start or expand the business.
- List of what resources (i.e., building, machinery, equipment, etc.)
- Explain how the costs of these resources will be financed.
- Create a management and personnel summary

Modern Thinking Tips

- There is no such thing as "out of the office" anymore. So now with the help of a wireless connection your office location can be anywhere.
- Equipment leasing is more of an option in this changing world as many creative suppliers pitch for your business... and it makes sense (cost wise as technology moves faster.

- Thanks to technology now you can consider virtual help for tasks from qualified people no matter where you are – Marketing support, Social media assistant, business development, etc.
- The "gig economy" of freelance workers has allowed employers to hire on demand, thus reducing costs for talent. (Source: fastcompany.com)

6. Product/Service Description, Market Research, Target and Competitive Analysis

Product/Service Description
This section of your business plan should give complete details on your product or services - and any variation to your industry. This gives the reader a clear understanding of what your company has to offer.

Your Market and Competitive Analysis
This section of your business plan should illustrate your industry and market knowledge as well as any of your

research findings and conclusions. This section is usually presented after the company description.

What to Include in Your Market Analysis

Industry Description and Outlook – Describe your industry, including its current size and historic growth rate as well as other trends and characteristics. Next, list the major customer groups within your industry.

Information About Your Target Market – Narrow your target market to a manageable size. Many businesses make the mistake of trying to appeal to too many target markets.

Research and include the following information:
Distinguishing characteristics – What are the critical needs of your potential customers? Are those needs being met? What are the demographics of the group and where

are they located? Are there any seasonal or cyclical purchasing trends that may impact your business?

Size of the primary target market – In addition to the size of your market, what data can you include about the annual purchases your market makes in your industry? What is the forecasted market growth for this group? For more information, search online for market research for tips and free government resources that can help you build a market profile.

In Review:
- Give complete details on your product or services.
- Illustrate your industry, outlook, and market knowledge.
- Supply information about your target market and size.
- List distinguishing characteristics and critical needs.

Modern Thinking Tips

- Messaging, branding, and today's corporate identity must address your competitive analysis that translates to value to the consumer.
- Utilize online research tools such as Ibisworld Industry Reports, Dun & Bradstreet research and advanced insights to get the current information you need.
- Equally important; Demographics explain "who" your buyer is, while psychographics explain "why" they buy.
- 63% of people don't realize they're already using Artificial Intelligence technologies. Use of voice search has seriously increased, so SEO and market researchers need to take notice.

Connecting Your
Business Plan

7. Pricing, Industry Trends, Marketing Plan and Marketing Budget Draft

Marketing Plan/Budget Draft

This section of your business plan should give complete details on your marketing strategy - and any variation to your industry. This gives the reader a clear understanding of how you'll get exposure in the marketplace.

What to Include in Your Marketing Plan

Marketing Timeline – Describe (list) your activities plan and how you'll take advantage of major opportunities to communicate with the customer.

Remember you are marketing to a manageable size. Many businesses make the same mistake of at first trying to market in too many areas. The timeline consists of activities that are free to utilize and some that cost on an ongoing basis. You can spend a million dollars on marketing with little success unless you're prepared to track results. Even then results can shift over time so be prepared to revise your marketing plan when needed.

Research data can also help in your decisions as to forecasted market growth for your industry. For more information, there are several free government resources that can help you build a marketing strategy including the US Census Bureau, the SBA Department, the Small Business Development, and Economic Development Centers in your area.

In Review:
- Illustrate your industry, market knowledge, and research findings and conclusions.
- Marketing Timeline – Describe (list) your activities plan and how you'll take advantage of major opportunities.
- Cover Your Target Market – Marketing to a manageable size.

Modern Thinking Tips
- When deciding where to focus your marketing research and strategy, look at customers' interests and determine where your company can fill gaps.
- Check into "Programmatic" ad buying in combination with hyper local (small community) targeting as a marketing tool. Programmatic pinpoints audiences on devices used the most.
- Live chat helps marketing efforts. In fact, the customer satisfaction rate is 73%, a lot higher than any other option.
- Mobile Advertising has changed the game for consumers and businesses alike. According to analyst estimates, by 2019, mobile display ads will account for nearly 40% of all digital display ads.

8. Projected Revenue and Expense Statement, Cash Flow Projections, and Break-even Analysis

Financial Statements

This section of your business plan support the three basic financial statements

1. Balance sheet – which shows firm's assets, liabilities, and net worth on a stated date.

2. Income statement – (profit & loss account).

3. Cash flow statement – which shows the inflows and outflows of cash caused by activities during a stated period.

Break-even Point

Illustrate your total expenses; where your costs may be at any given point. And where sales volume should be at your break-even point based on you market research assumptions and conclusions.

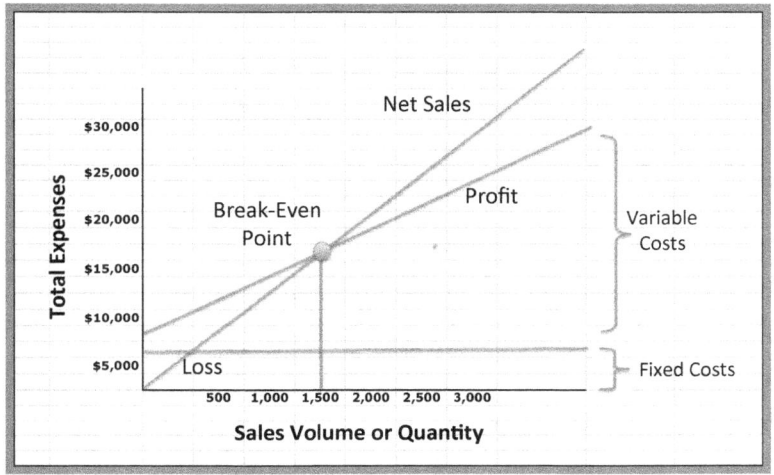

Balance Sheet: When researching various balance sheet templates, here are a couple of definitions to clarify:

Defining "Capital Stock"
Capital is defined as the total dollars a company receives to operate the business. Capital can be obtained by issuing stock (equity) or debt securities. Companies with consistent corporate profits raise more firm capital by issuing debt, because the firm can generate income to make interest payments.

Sample Small Business Balance Sheet[0]			
Assets		**Liabilities and Owners' Equity**	
Cash	$ 16,600	Liabilities:	
Accounts Receivable	1,200	Notes Payable	$ 30,000
Land	52,000	Accounts Payable	7,000
Building	36,000	Total liabilities	$ 37,000
Tools and equipment	12,000	Owners' equity:	
		Capital Stock	$ 80,000
		Retained Earnings	800
			80,800
Total	$117,800	Total	$117,800

What are "Retained Earnings?"

Retained earnings refer to the percentage of net earnings not paid out as dividends, but retained by the company to be reinvested in its core business, or to pay debt.

Cash-flow Statement

A cash flow financial statement shows how changes in balance sheet accounts and income affect cash and cash equivalents. It also breaks the analysis of operating the business at any point in time, how investing and financing activities are affected as well. There are several online spreadsheet templates to help get started in building a statement.

In Review:

- Draft your three basic financial statements: 1. Balance sheet, 2. Income statement and, 3. Cash flow statement, based on research findings and conclusions.
- Illustrate on draft as to where your costs may be at any given point, and where sales volume should be at break-even point.

Modern Thinking Tips

- Nowadays businesses are looking more at additional revenue streams to fill the gaps in uncertain times.
- Find ways to increase productivity to offset labor costs: 72% of small-business employees now say an improvement in their benefits offerings would make them even happier. (Source: Aflac 2017)
- Managing hidden costs, like training. With online competition, it takes an average of 27 days to hire

a new employee. The best candidates are off the market within 10 days. (Source: Undercover Recruiter)

- That in mind, modern training tools such as webinars, video conferencing and communication can encourage new employees feel more secure and productive.

Driving Ecommerce Revenue in a Modern World

1. Retailers and restaurants are using services such as Groupon and Foursquare to attract new customers.

2. 90% of a consumer's time is spent on mobile apps... not mobile browsers. Getting the right app is a big investment but worth it.

3. The #1 reason for shopping cart abandonment rates being as high as 67% are shipping costs increasing the total price. 81% of customers say they are more likely to make a purchase if an ecommerce business offers free shipping.

4. Around 83% of customers agree that they need support in order to complete a purchase. So Live chat is believed to be the best way to get in touch with customers.

5. Around 50% of users abandon a purchase because they feel insecure about sharing their private details, including personal information. The solution is to use the right cart that is not only easy to use but also safe.

Connecting Your
Business Plan

9. The Road to Financing: Summary of Financial Needs, Financial Records, and Business/Personal Credit Report

6 Things To Know About The Presentation of Financial Statements

1. Financial Statements Are Scorecards

Investors seek out quality companies with strong balance sheets, solid earnings and positive cash flow. Whether you're a do-it-yourself or rely on guidance from a professional, learning certain fundamental financial statement analysis skills can be very useful. Overly complex statistical analysis and formulas that don't convey information any better than straight talk about your business.

2. What Financial Statements to Use

For analysis purposes, the financial statements used are the balance sheet, the income statement, the cash flow statement as well as shareholders'/owners equity and

36

retained earnings. In the best of circumstances, management should be scrupulously honest and candid.

3. Know What's Behind the Numbers
The numbers in a company's financials reflect real world events. These numbers and the financial ratios/indicators for analysis are easier to understand if you can visualize the underlying realities of this essentially quantitative information.

4. The Challenge of Understanding Financial Jargon
The lack of any appreciable standardization of financial reporting terminology complicates the understanding of many financial statement account entries. Keep in mind this circumstance can be confusing for an investor, financial institution, etc.

5. Non-Financial Statement Information
Information on the state of the economy, industry and competitive considerations, market forces, technological change, and the quality of management and the workforce are not directly reflected in a company's financial statements. Investors need to recognize that financial statement insights are but one piece, although an important one, of the larger investment information puzzle.

6. Financial Ratios and Indicators
The absolute numbers in financial statements are of little value for investment analysis. Numbers should transform into meaningful relationships to judge a company's financial performance and condition. Beware, for one-size-fits-all syndrome that evaluative financial metrics can differ significantly by industry, company size and stage of development.

Sample of Start-up Expense Worksheet

One Time Start Up Expenses	Amount	Notes
Advertising and promotion		
Buildout/Renovations		
Cash for Operations		
Consulting Fees		
Decorating Painting and Remodeling		
Deposits and Public Utilities		
Equipment		
Furniture and Fixtures		
Legal and Professional Fees		
License and Permits		
One Time Start Up Costs		
Rent Deposit		
Software		
Starting Inventory		
Misc:		
Other:		
Total One Time Start Up Costs		

Sample of Monthly Expense Worksheet

Monthly Expenses	Amount	Notes
Bank Charges		
Debt Service (Principal and Interest)		
Insurance		
Maintenance and Repairs		
Marketing and Promotion: Ad		
Marketing and Promotion: Other		
Membership and Dues		
Misc:		
Payroll Tax		
Payroll: Wages (Employees)		
Payroll: Wages (Owner/Manager)		
Professional Fees: Accounting		
Professional Fees: Other		
Rent		
Subscriptions		
Supplies		
Telephone		
Utilities		
Other		
Total Mothly Expenses		
Number of months estimated to cover Expenses		

Here are Links to Online Spreadsheet Templates

Start-up Cost Spreadsheet
https://www.score.org/resource/start-expenses

Financial Projections Spreadsheet
https://www.score.org/resource/financial-projections-template

In Review:

- Draft a presentation that covers the 6 things to know about financial statements.
- Create a start-up cost spreadsheet (utilizing template).
- Illustrate assumptions as to where your sales/costs and cash flow may be with a financial projections spreadsheet (utilizing template).
- If financing is required, inquire into your business/personal credit history to start and discuss further with your bank.

Modern Thinking Tips

- Secure File Sharing and Storage Solutions offering online cloud storage, file synchronization, business records cloud, and integrated client software now moves information faster.
- Innovation and diversification is key. The greatest challenge to small business growth and survival is economic uncertainty, followed closely by lower consumer spending and regulatory burdens. (Source: (NSBA) National Small Business Association)
- Nowadays businesses turn more so to alternative funding. Big banks only approved around 24.1% of small business loans. Smaller banks have a much higher approval rate of around 48.9%. Alternative Lenders approved 58.2% of loan requests. (Source: Biz2Credit 2017)

10. Drafting your Plan, Setting a Timetable, Key Contacts, Resumes, Marketing Materials, etc.

Following a timetable in essential in allowing the reader of you plan to understand what your business is all about. Displaying confidence in planning your strategy is important, not only for your investors or lenders but also your landlord when negotiating a lease agreement and ultimately your loyal "soon to be" customers.

Drafting: The key components of your Business Plan.
Follow these 10 specific steps below when drafting your business plan. Spend the time reviewing and editing what you've come up with to ensure you have clearly made your points. The business model and concept you assemble is essentially your "dog and pony show," so with that in mind, you'll want to make a great first impression.

Business Resources and Related Information

U.S. Census Bureau
Small Business Development Centers (SBDC)
Small Business Administration (SBA)
Business Information Center (BIC)
Women's Business Centers (WBCs)
Minority Business Centers (MBCs)
University and Community libraries
SCORE
Trade associations
Suppliers and vendors

Local business mentoring groups
Local chamber of commerce
Local nonprofit foundations
Local or state office of Economic Development
Local credit union or community bank
Magazines and newspapers
Business websites. expert blogs
Talking with potential customers
Talking with competitors

So There You Have It!
Guiding you on the best road to a business plan!

Connecting Your Business Plan to a Modern World

Business Plan Tips in Review

1. Draft a Business Summary of Ideas and Overviews
2. The Business Name and the Executive Summary
3. Your Mission Statement, Goals and Objectives
4. Tips on Legal Structure, Permits/Licenses, and Insurance
5. Tips on Operations, Facility/Location, Equipment, Management/Personnel

6. Building a Marketing Plan: Product/Service Description, Market Research, Target, and Competitive Analysis
7. Tips on a Marketing Plan Budget: Pricing, Industry Trends, Marketing Costs
8. Creating a Financial Plan: Projected Revenue and Expense Statement, Cash Flow Projections, Break-even Analysis
9. The Road to Financing: Summary of Financial Needs, Historical Financial Records, and Business/Personal Credit Report
10. Drafting your Plan, Setting a Timetable, Key Contacts, Resumes, Marketing Materials, etc.

Various Sources also include: Economic Trends and Research Data, Conference Board of Canada, and United States, U.S. Bureau of Labor and Statistics, Learning & Development Outlook Report, International Workplace Education, Wikipedia, the free encyclopedia, Training Studies and Tested Field Experience.

About the Author

John DeGaetano – *on the business side, John is a certified business advisor and instructor and works with many businesses in guiding them in creating economic impact in the form of sales, jobs, retaining jobs, market analysis, and planning. He makes presentations on a variety of subjects.*

On the artistic side, John is the artistic director of a theatre company non-profit organization and author of several full length and 10-minute plays. His stage director credits include; Cats, Pirates of Penzance, Joseph and the Amazing Technicolor Dreamcoat, Chicago, West Side Story, and Evita to name a few. He's assisted with numerous other productions such as Miss Saigon along with Radio and Television work. His plays, informational books and presentations are available on Amazon, bookstores, and elsewhere.

John DeGaetano Productions

More titles in the
"How to" and "10 Ridiculously Simple Tips" Series

Includes:
How to Write a Business Plan
Creative Ways to Fund Your Small Business
Audition for the Stage
Financial Projections
Marketing
Motivation
Writing a Resume
Sales
Social Networking
Stage Production
Training